Pop the Pot on

Written by Holly Woolnough
Illustrated by Lee Holland

Collins

T0327875

Get a red pot.

Pop it on top.

Go, get the tin.

Rip the top.

rip

The pot is hot.

Tip it up and in.

Get the hot mug.

Dip it. Tip it in.

Pop on a sun hat.

Sit on the red rug.

Run the tap. Tip it.

Pop it on the rack.

/r/

14

After reading

Letters and Sounds: Phase 2

Word count: 54

Focus phonemes: /g/ /o/ /c/ ck /e/ /u/ /r/ /h/

Common exception words: the, and, go, is

Curriculum links: Personal, social and emotional development

Early learning goals: Reading: read and understand simple sentences; use phonic knowledge to decode regular words and read them aloud accurately; read some irregular words

Developing fluency

- Your child may enjoy hearing you read the book.
- Take turns to read a page, demonstrating how to read with expression. Check your child pauses at full stops, and at the comma on page 4.

Phonic practice

- Turn to pages 2 and 3 and point to **pot**. Ask your child to sound out and blend the letters. (*p/o/t – **pot***) Can they find a word with the same /o/ sound on page 3? (*pop, top*)
- Take turns to point out a word for each other to sound out and blend. For one turn, point to **rack** on page 13, and check your child remembers that "ck" makes one sound.
- Look at the "I spy sounds" pages (14 and 15). Point to the /r/ and /h/ at the corners of the pages and sound them out. Say: I can see some things that begin with the /r/ sound. Point to the tennis racket and say "racket", emphasising the /r/ sound. Support your child in finding more /r/ words (*rack, rabbit, rainbow, red, running*). Then look for /h/ words together (*hat, handbag, hedge, hula hoop, horse, helmet*).

Extending vocabulary

- Look at each double page again and take turns to say what a character is doing, starting the sentence with: He is … / She is … . Point out how we don't know the children's names so we can use "he" or "she" instead.